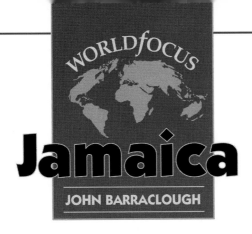

WORLD*FOCUS*

Jamaica

JOHN BARRACLOUGH

Contents

Note to the Reader
Some words in this book are printed in **bold** type. This shows that the word is listed in the glossary on page 30. The glossary gives a brief explanation of words that might be new to you.

Introduction

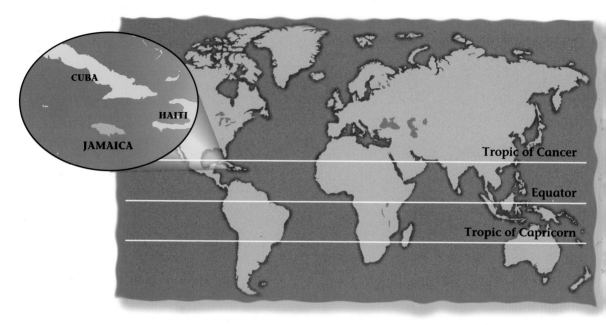

Jamaica is one of the islands in the Caribbean. Some people think it is shaped like a turtle, swimming between the United States and South America. The island is 146 miles long, from west to east, and 51 miles at its widest point, from north to south. Jamaica covers an area of about 4,243 square miles, which is about half the size of the state of Massachusetts. More than eight times the number of people live on one square mile of land in Jamaica as on the same area in the United States. This means that Jamaica has a much higher population density.

Where is Jamaica?

Climate

A ridge of mountains divides Jamaica along its middle. The land is greener and more fertile to the north of the mountains, where the winds off the ocean drop their rain. Most of the island's bananas are grown here. The south of Jamaica is drier than the north. Sugar cane grows well here on flat land by the side of rivers. Jamaica lies in a hurricane zone. In 1988 the worst Caribbean storm in this century hit the island. In only a few hours Hurricane Gilbert destroyed thousands of buildings and caused massive damage and flooding.

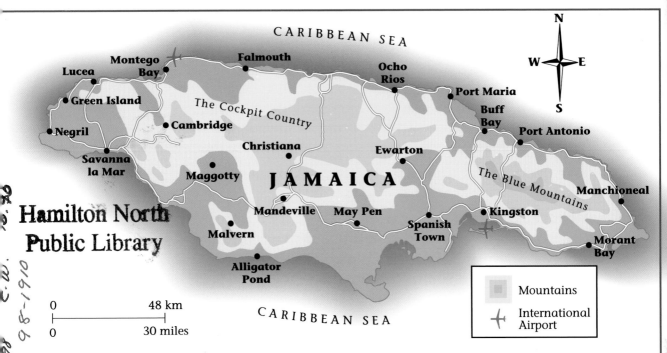

CARIBBEAN SEA

Lucea
Montego Bay
Falmouth
Ocho Rios
Port Maria
Buff Bay
Port Antonio

Green Island

The Cockpit Country

Negril

Cambridge

Christiana

Ewarton

The Blue Mountains

Manchioneal

Savanna la Mar

Maggotty

JAMAICA

Mandeville
May Pen
Kingston

Malvern
Spanish Town
Morant Bay

Alligator Pond

CARIBBEAN SEA

▢	Mountains
✈	International Airport

0   48 km

0   30 miles

 The main features of Jamaica.

 **Jamaica is one of the most beautiful islands in the Caribbean.**

Jamaica's banana crop was very badly damaged, and it has only recently recovered.

Behind Jamaica's capital city, Kingston, the mountains reach nearly 7,900 feet which is higher than the tallest mountain in the Appalachians. Jamaica is in the tropics and is hot all year round. During the day clouds form over the mountains behind Kingston, and the mountains look blue. This is how they got their name, the Blue Mountains. The coffee that grows here is the best quality and most expensive coffee in the world. Very few Jamaicans can afford to buy it. Blue Mountain coffee is **exported** to Europe, North America, and Japan.

Poverty

Rich people and poor people in Jamaica have very different lives. A small number of very rich families owns most of the land and can buy whatever they want or need to be comfortable. But for many people, life is hard. One-third of Jamaicans live in poverty. They struggle to afford decent housing, healthy food, or medicine when they fall ill.

3

The People

The first people to live on Jamaica were the Arawak Indians. They lived in small villages in huts made from palm leaves. They grew crops and raised animals and were good sailors. Today there are no Arawaks left.

Slavery

The explorer Christopher Columbus arrived in Jamaica in 1494. Spanish **colonists** followed him and introduced bananas and sugar cane to the island. These settlers made the Arawaks work on their farms and treated them very cruelly. Many died from overwork and starvation, and from European diseases to which they had no resistance. In only 20 years the Arawaks had all died out. Then the Spanish brought black people from Africa to work for them as slaves. The slave trade grew quickly and was mostly run by the British, who later took control of Jamaica from the Spanish.

One-third of the population of Jamaica is under 15 years old.

British slave traders shipped men, women, and children from Africa to Jamaica and other countries in the Caribbean. On these long voyages up to half the slaves died from overcrowding and disease. The survivors were sold in Jamaica at Kingston market to rich plantation owners for very little money.

The slaves regularly fought back against their harsh owners, and there were revolts and escapes. Resistance to rule by white people spread and was passed from generation to generation. Eventually it helped Jamaica to leave the British Empire, and in 1962 the country became independent. But today, as in the days of slavery, most of the land in Jamaica is owned by a handful of very powerful families and businesses.

Religion

Jamaica has more churches per square mile than any other country in the world. Church is very important to many people, particularly in villages, where church social events can be big occasions for the community.

Jamaica is the home of the Rastafarian religion. Some believers, or Rastas, grow their hair into thick ropes called dreadlocks. True Rastas are peace-loving and do not eat meat. The Rastafarian movement began in Jamaica in the 1930s when Rastas started to live together in groups, or communes. They believe in a simple, back-to-nature lifestyle and call on black people to be proud of their African ancestry. The most famous Rastafarian was Bob Marley, the **reggae** musician.

△ Most Jamaicans are descended from Africans brought to the island to be slaves 400 years ago. Mr. Owen "O.G." Davies is a member of the Rastafarian religion.

▲ There is a housing shortage in Jamaica because land is very expensive.

Jamaica has a population of 2.5 million, and the same number of Jamaicans lives in other countries. Finding a job is difficult in Jamaica, and many young people leave the island to find work in the United States, Canada, and the United Kingdom.

In the 1950s, large numbers of Jamaicans were encouraged by the British government to **emigrate** to Britain to help rebuild the country after World War II. They were willing to work hard and take jobs that were often low-paid, such as nursing and factory work. Today, London and Birmingham, England, are centers of Jamaican **culture**. Many families in Jamaica depend on money sent to them by their relatives living abroad.

Cities

Almost half of Jamaica's people live in the four main cities on the island: Kingston, Spanish Town, Montego Bay, and May Pen. Kingston is the capital and is the biggest by far. Over 600,000 people live there.

Kingston is growing as more and more people come to the city from the countryside, looking for jobs. The other towns are growing too, and there is a shortage of housing because land is very expensive.

New arrivals at the cities often end up living in slum areas on the outskirts, called shanties. They have no electricity, clean water, or **sanitation**. Shanty houses are built from whatever people can get hold of: corrugated iron, packing crates, or plastic sheeting. The land that people live on but do not own or pay rent for is called "captured" land in Jamaica. One-third of Jamaicans live on captured land.

▽ The best houses in Kingston are on the slopes of the Blue Mountains. Most of them have satellite dishes.

The Countryside

In the countryside most people make their living either by farming or by working on the sugar or banana plantations. Many plantation workers also grow a few bananas and vegetables in their backyards or on spare land. These are to eat or to sell at market. A trip to market can involve getting up before dawn to catch the bus to the nearest town. People often sleep overnight at the market until they have sold all their produce. Sugar and banana plantations employ large numbers of workers, but there still aren't enough jobs to go around.

Agriculture

In Jamaica, many types of fruit and vegetable grow well. There is sun and rain all year round, and the soil is fertile, though nutrients in the soil can be washed out by heavy rain. The best land for crops is the flat areas by the rivers. But because Jamaica is a small and hilly island, there is limited space for big fields. The mountain soils are thin, and the fields are steep and difficult to farm. Coffee grows well here because it is cooler.

Sugar and Bananas

Jamaica's most important crop is sugar cane. It is a type of grass that grows up to sixteen feet tall. When the cane fields are ready to harvest, they are burned to get rid of the weeds. The cane itself does not burn. The men who cut the cane are paid for each ton they harvest. On a good day they can cut two tons a day. But when the wind is in the wrong direction, it can tangle the cane and make it very difficult to cut. Then the men don't earn very much. The juice from the cane is made into sugar and rum.

In the 1970s the sugar estates were owned by the government and run by the workers. In the 1980s, the government sold the estates to big companies. They argue that to make profits, they must keep costs low, so the wages of the cane cutters have fallen.

Bananas are another important crop. Half the bananas grown there are exported. They are grown by farmers on small plots of land and on big plantations owned by companies and the government. Bananas need **irrigation** and **fertilizer** to grow well. Plantation owners can afford these agricultural techniques, but most small farmers cannot. On plantations, men do the irrigation work, and it is usually women's work to put fertilizer around the stems of the plants. As with most jobs in Jamaica and other parts of the world, men are paid more than women.

△ Loading up sugar cane onto trucks.

▷ One-fifth of Jamaicans work in agriculture.

Each week a ship leaves the island, carrying refrigerated green bananas to Europe. When they arrive, they are put into storage. There they ripen and turn yellow before they are sold in markets and supermarkets.

One-fifth of Jamaicans work in agriculture and fishing. Many work on sugar estates or banana plantations. Some rent small farms, and a few have their own land.

Debt and Hurricanes

The government used to lend money to farmers to improve their farms. But now the government owes a lot of money to other countries. They have had to make cutbacks and cannot give the farmers as many loans. Now it is much harder for poor farmers to make a living.

In 1988 a hurricane called Hurricane Gilbert hit Jamaica. It did a lot of damage. Most of the banana plants and many coffee bushes were destroyed. But sugar cane survived because it bends in the wind. Jamaican agriculture has not fully recovered from Hurricane Gilbert.

Industry

Jamaica is hot all year round. It has beautiful scenery, sandy beaches and warm sea. People like to go on vacation there, and tourism has become Jamaica's biggest industry. The government encourages local people to run their own small hotels and guest houses, and the island's biggest hotel chain is owned by Jamaicans. Other tourist hotels are often owned by big foreign companies that have hotels all over the world.

Many young Jamaicans work in the hotels as waiters and housekeeping staff. People also make money by selling food and handicrafts to tourists on the beach. A lot of the jobs in the tourist industry are **seasonal**. Most American and Canadian tourists visit Jamaica in December and January, when it is cold at home. People can lose their jobs when there are not so many tourists.

△ **Hotels are built on some of the best land.**

Bauxite

In the hills of Jamaica there are bauxite mines. Bauxite is the raw material from which aluminum is made. Aluminum is used to make many things—from cans to airplanes. The bauxite is like sticky red-brown soil and is sometimes called "red gold." It is dug up using mechanical diggers that can fill a 50-ton truck in less than five minutes. It takes only a few days to dig a bauxite mine the size of a football stadium. The bauxite goes by train to Ocho Rios on the north coast. Then bulk carrier ships transport it to North America, where it is made into aluminum.

△ **Some bauxite mines are so big, they can be seen from space.**

The land with the best bauxite is owned by American and Canadian companies. When these companies bought the land, they had to give the people who lived there some money to move away. Most families took the money and moved. But a few people didn't want to leave their houses. Today they are surrounded by bauxite mines. The mines are also a problem because they can pollute people's drinking water.

Like many countries, Jamaica owes a lot of money to other countries. It uses the money it makes from tourism and the bauxite industry to pay some of its debts. Jamaica could make more money if it sold aluminum abroad instead of bauxite. But **smelting** bauxite to make aluminum takes lots of electricity and expensive equipment, such as furnaces. Jamaica cannot afford these.

Challenges

As with other developing countries, one of the biggest problems facing Jamaica is debt. It owes money to other countries and to banks. To pay some of these debts, Jamaica has had to cut spending. So the government has spent less money on schools and hospitals. Families also now have to pay to send their children to school and have to pay the doctor if they are ill. At the same time **inflation** is high, and so the cost of food and transportation keeps going up. Life has become more difficult for poor people, especially poor women.

▷ Health services have been cut. Some communities have started their own clinics, like this one.

Women

About one-third of families in Jamaica are cared for by women who are on their own. Often they get no help from their husbands or the father of the children in the family. Typically, the women have more responsibility, more work, and less money than men. Even so, women are influential in Jamaican **society**. Ever since the time of slavery, they have joined together to try to improve their lives.

Health

In a poor area of Kingston a group of women is improving the health of their children. Oxfam and another **development agency** are helping them by providing some training in **primary health care**. This care aims to keep people healthy so they do not need to go to the doctor. The women teach each other about the importance of **sanitation**. They also check that each child in the community is **vaccinated** against childhood diseases, such as measles.

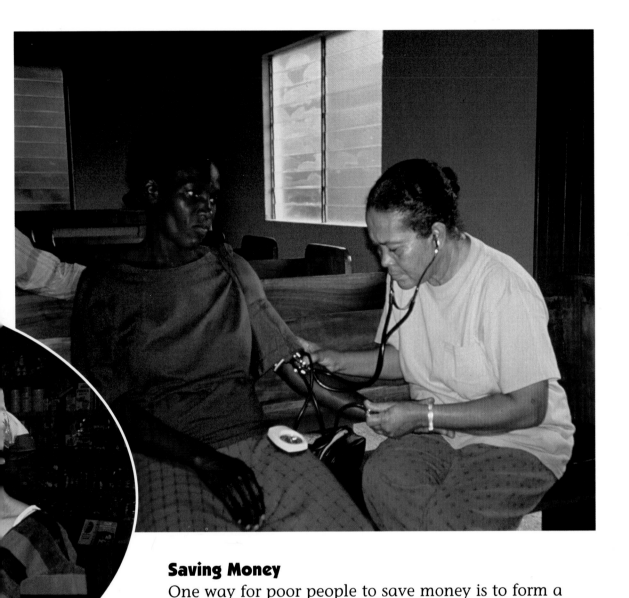

△ **High inflation makes life difficult, especially for poor women who are caring for their families on their own.**

Saving Money

One way for poor people to save money is to form a savings club. This is called a partner system. There may be up to 20 partners in one club. The club members choose a person to be banker. The banker collects a few Jamaican dollars from each partner every month and keeps the money safe. The partners then have meetings to decide who in the club should receive a payment, and when. That way people know when they will get a payment and can plan how to spend it. Savings clubs are a good way to save money for expensive things like school fees, concrete to build houses, or a second-hand car.

Montego Bay is Jamaica's second-biggest city. It is on the northwest coast of the island. About 85,000 people live there. Montego Bay is a busy port, and many tourists arrive here first when they visit Jamaica. They come either by cruise ship from the United States, or by airplane to Montego Bay's international airport. Flights arrive here from all over the world. It takes about nine hours to fly from London and less than two hours from Florida.

Tourism

Montego Bay is growing in population and is spreading as people build new houses on the outskirts of the city. Many young people come to Montego Bay from the country, looking for jobs. They hope to get work in the tourist industry, perhaps working in one of the many hotels. But these jobs are difficult to get, even though they are low paid.

There are hotels in the center of Montego Bay and along the coast on the beach. Some tourists who visit Jamaica are happy to stay on the beach, enjoying the sunshine. Some people don't even leave their hotel to see what the country is like, and the only Jamaicans they meet are hotel staff and taxi drivers.

The Jamaican government encourages tourism because tourists bring money to the island. But many hotels are owned by foreign companies. These companies take their money out of the country. So Jamaica does not get all the money the tourists spend. Hotels and their golf courses are often built on some of the best agricultural land—flat, with deep soil. When a new hotel is built, the land can no longer be used to grow fruit and vegetables. The farmers who worked on the land also lose their jobs. Finding a new job in Jamaica is difficult because **unemployment** is high.

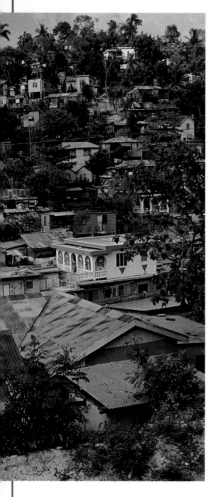

△ Montego Bay is growing as people come to the city to look for jobs.

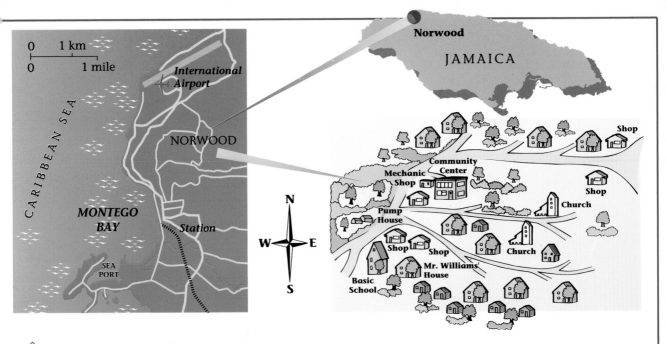

Montego Bay and the suburb of Norwood.

Norwood

Norwood is a **suburb** on the edge of Montego Bay. About 8,000 people live there. Many families came to Norwood in the 1970s, when lots of hotels were being built around Montego Bay. People got jobs as building laborers and hotel workers. Now most people who move to Norwood are from Montego Bay. They leave the city center because rents there are high. The people who move to Norwood build their own small houses, or they live with friends and relatives. Some houses are made from wood, others from brick or concrete blocks. Almost every house has bars on the windows to stop burglars from breaking in.

Houses in the poorer part of the city often have no running water of their own.

15

Life in Norwood

Norwood **suburb** is the size of a small town. It is built on a hill overlooking Montego Bay airport. Even though 8,000 people live in Norwood, there are few services. Not everybody has electricity or water, and garbage is collected only in some streets. Legally, the people of Norwood have no right to live there. The land is owned by the government or by big landowners.

Many of the people who live in Norwood came here because they heard there were jobs in Montego Bay. They built small wooden houses on Norwood's unused land. When they had some money, they replaced the wood with bricks or concrete blocks.

▽ The Williams family outside their home in Norwood.

The Williams Family

The Williams family came to Norwood in 1978. They moved onto a small, steep plot of land squeezed between other houses. In Jamaica this is called "capturing" land. People on captured land have no security and can be **evicted** at any time.

The Williams' first house was made of wood. It burned down in 1982. Since then Mr. Uriah Williams has been rebuilding the family's new house out of concrete and rock. He is digging into the side of the hill to make the foundations of the house.

▷ Building their home takes most of the Williams family's money.

Then he uses the rock he removes to make walls. Mr. Williams plans to have nine rooms in the house. There are ten people in the family. So far he has finished two rooms. There are walls for two more rooms, but they have no roofs and cannot be lived in yet. Mr. Williams and his wife, Mrs. Millicent Williams, are saving to buy cement and beams to put the roof on a third room.

Building the house is slow because the Williams can only afford to build one room at a time. They can only buy building materials if there is any money left over after they have paid their children's school fees and bought school uniforms. Children cannot go to school without a uniform. They believe it is more important to send their children to school than to finish the house.

School

There are no schools in Norwood because the government will not build a school on captured land. Children from Norwood have to travel into Montego Bay to go to school. The Williams children share a taxi into town. Dennis Williams, who is eight years old, goes to a **church school**. There are many church schools in Jamaica and lots of churches.

School System

When Jamaica became independent from Britain in 1962, it built many schools. They followed the British educational system, using British books and exams.

Jamaica faces problems with its educational system. One reason is that one-third of all Jamaicans are under 15 years old. Educating so many people is expensive. Recently the government has had to make cuts in spending on education because of debts abroad. Some people blame the cuts for the growing number of children who cannot read or write. If young people cannot read or write when they leave school, they find it very difficult to get a job. Most of the factories in Kingston and Montego Bay will only employ people who are **literate** and **numerate**.

◁ Children who go to preschool learn to read and write earlier.

▽ More girls go to college than boys.

Preschools

In Jamaica small children between three and six years old can go to nursery school, known as preschool, if their parents can pay. But the government has had to cut back on these schools. Teachers are now paid so little that some cannot afford to be teachers anymore. They can get paid more money doing other jobs, even though they trained to be teachers. Almost all teachers in Jamaica are women, and many are looking for jobs abroad.

Some preschools have closed. Others are sponsored by churches, businesses, or local people. In one parish in the west of Jamaica, six villages have sponsored their preschools. The communities get some money from Oxfam, and they raise the rest themselves. The money is used to pay the teachers and to buy desks, books, paper, and pencils. It is important for young children to go to preschool. If they don't, it takes them longer to learn to read and write when they go to primary school.

Spare Time

A game called cricket is very popular in Jamaica. Young people, mainly boys, play it from an early age using a soft ball, a piece of wood for the bat, and sticks for the stumps. They will play on any spare piece of ground. Cricket matches are played all over the island, especially on Sunday afternoons. They are very competitive. There are usually some Jamaican players on the famous **West Indies** cricket team. When the West Indies team plays another national team, like England or Australia, people all over Jamaica listen to the cricket broadcast on the radio.

Cricket is still the most popular sport, but now lots of people play soccer as well. More and more families have satellite TV and are able to pick up sports and other programs from the United States. Basketball has become popular with young Jamaicans, partly because many of the most successful players are African Americans.

▽ **Young cricketers make their own bats and wickets.**

Athletics

Jamaica has produced some world-class athletes, such as Don Quarrie in the 1970s and Merlene Ottey, the 200-meter sprinter. The achievements of these athletes are something that young people, particularly girls and women, can look up to and aim for. For poor young athletes a sports **scholarship** to the United States can be an escape from poverty.

The United States is only two hours away by air, and many Jamaicans have visited or worked there. American sports, fashions, food, and music have become very popular in Jamaica. Some older people are worried that Jamaican **culture** is being pushed to one side. In Kingston and other towns, young people often paint walls with **murals** of their heroes. In the past they were always Jamaican. Now they are also American.

 Young Jamaicans follow American fashion and culture. The Chicago Bulls basketball team is part of this mural.

Music

The reggae singer Bob Marley, who died in 1978, is a major hero in Jamaica and the rest of the world. Reggae, dub, and ragga have influenced pop music all over the world.

Music is a very important part of Jamaican life. People enjoy playing music, and listening and dancing to it. On weekends there are dances and concerts all over the island—in towns, in the country, and on the beach. Some are held in special dance halls. Others are set up in the open air, where huge speakers are used. Music events usually start in the evening. People of all ages eat, drink, and dance together.

A Day with the Williamses

The Williams family lives in Norwood on the edge of Montego Bay. The ten of them live together in two small rooms in the house built by Mr. Williams. Mr. and Mrs. Williams share a bedroom, and the rest of the family lives in the room next door. Almost all the space is taken up by beds pushed together. Clothes are hung from hooks on the wall. So are a cassette player and a radio. There are books on the window ledges and a picture of the Jamaican flag on the wall. Like many Jamaicans, the Williamses are a **patriotic** family.

Morning

The family's day begins just after dawn. Dennis is eight years old. He gets up about 7 A.M. and has a breakfast of cereal and milk. Mrs. Williams makes tea for all the family. She uses a small hotplate in the entrance to the house. It is very cramped.

Dennis has to get water from the faucet at the back of the house every day. He also feeds the chickens and collects their eggs. Many families in Jamaica keep chickens and goats in their yards, even in the towns. People also grow a few vegetables to eat or to sell.

▽ Mr. Williams making the rugs that Mrs. Williams sells at her stall in Montego Bay.

Dennis and several other children share a taxi to school in Montego Bay. When they have gone, Mrs. Williams goes to work. She rents a stall by the roadside in the center of Montego Bay. Here she sells hats and rugs to tourists. The rugs are made by Mr. Williams.

Mr. Williams spends his day making mats or doing jobs for other people, such as gardening or electrical work. He finds it difficult to work these days because he fell and hurt his knee. At first he used a **traditional** cure for his injury. He wrapped his knee in the leaves of a local fruit, the custard apple, soaked in vinegar. When this didn't work, he spent five days in the hospital. The hospital bill was equal to what Mr. Williams earns in two weeks.

Evening

When Mrs. Williams gets home, she cooks for the family while Dennis does his homework. Everybody eats together. Most days they will have rice and kidney beans. Jamaicans call this rice 'n' peas. It is eaten with lots of different vegetables, or a hot and spicy sauce, or meat, such as chicken or pork.

After dinner the children soon go to bed. Then Mr. or Mrs. Williams might go to the community center. It gets dark by 8:00 P.M. and everybody is in bed by 10:00 P.M.

△ Mr. Williams with his son Dennis and granddaughter, Kerry-Anne.

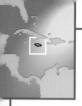

Traveling in Norwood

Most of the people who live in Norwood commute into Montego Bay every day for work. If they have a short journey, people will walk or go by bicycle. For longer journeys, they will catch a bus. Jamaican buses are very crowded and uncomfortable. To be sure of getting a seat, some commuters even catch the bus before it is light in the morning.

Free Zones

Many women from Norwood work in the Free Zone in Montego Bay. This is an industrial park on the other side of the city. The Jamaican government has encouraged foreign companies to set up their businesses here. This brings money into Jamaica and helps to pay the country's debt. The government has made it easy for the companies in the Free Zone. They pay low taxes and low wages for their workers. **Unions** are not allowed in the Free Zone, so the workers cannot get together to ask for better wages and working conditions.

▽ Many women from Norwood commute to the Free Zone to work.

△ Some banana estate and sugar plantation workers are picked up by truck early in the morning to go to work.

Most of the people who work in the Free Zone are women. Their jobs are repetitive and boring. Even so, people want to work in the Free Zone because jobs are hard to find.

Most of the Free Zone workers go home by bus. Some factories have their own company buses that take people into the center of Montego Bay. There they catch buses or taxis home, or they walk. As in many other countries, there is a rush hour in Jamaica. Between 5:00 and 7:00 P.M. the roads are choked with traffic.

Cars

Cars are very expensive in Jamaica. Most of the cars in Jamaica made before 1970 are British, because Jamaica was a British colony. Almost all the newer cars are Japanese, German, or American. They all have to be **imported**. The charge to bring a car into Jamaica is as much as the price of the car. This extra amount is called import duty. It is a type of tax. Only wealthy Jamaicans can afford to buy a new car.

Journeys

Jamaica has a good road system covering most of the island. A main coast road circles the island, connecting the major towns like Kingston and Spanish Town. There are stretches of highways, but not expressways. Most roads are paved, except those in the most remote villages in the mountains. People drive fast in Jamaica, and not everyone has a driver's license. Accidents are reported nearly every day on the radio and in the newspapers. There are traffic jams in Kingston and other cities, just like there are in cities throughout the world.

Buses

Most Jamaicans travel by bus. Jamaica used to have a good bus service, owned and run by the government. The buses ran on a timetable and could be relied upon. Recently the government sold the buses to raise money. When a government sells an industry to private businesses, it is called privatization. The new owners began to compete for passengers, and they stopped using timetables. Travelers complain that the bus system is chaotic now. Buses are unreliable, more expensive, and very crowded.

▽ **You can fly from one side of Jamaica to the other in half an hour.**

▲ The older cars in Jamaica are mostly British.

Trains

Jamaica has a few railroad lines, but most of the trains carry freight, not passengers. The trains that run from the bauxite mines in the center of the island were built specially by the bauxite companies. They just transport bauxite to the ports, where it is loaded onto ships.

Gasoline is expensive in Jamaica because it has to be imported. Sometimes a garage will sell gasoline cheaper than anyone else to get more business. When this happens, drivers will line up to get the cheap fuel. A garage owner in Montego Bay who lowered his prices was threatened by other garage owners. They were afraid of losing business.

Jamaica has two main airports and a few airstrips used by light aircraft. It takes 30 minutes to fly across the island from Kingston to Montego Bay.

Street traders in Jamaica are called higglers and are usually women. The most successful ones often fly to Florida or New York to buy things like clothes and shoes to sell in Jamaica. They travel in groups called posses.

Looking at Jamaica

When you think about Jamaica, you might imagine a beautiful island of forested hills and sandy beaches, where tourists go on vacations. Or you may think of cricket, or rastas with their dreadlocks, or the reggae music of Bob Marley. This is the Jamaica you might see in a travel brochure or on television. But this book has tried to show you that there are other sides to Jamaica.

It is a country of great natural wealth. But while some people own houses with swimming pools and lots of land, many Jamaicans find it difficult to afford to send their children to school.

Almost any type of fruit or vegetable can be grown in Jamaica's tropical climate, but people still go hungry.

Bauxite, the source of aluminum, ought to make Jamaica rich. Instead, Jamaica is struggling. One reason is that it owes so much money to other countries. Another is that the price of its exports is decided by what other countries will pay, and sometimes Jamaica gets only a small amount for what it produces.

In the past, Jamaicans have suffered under a system of slavery. Today, the problems are different. The gap between rich landowners and poor landless farmers and poor city people is getting bigger.

Poor Jamaicans have joined together to organize and improve their lives. Some are buying their own land, getting better health care, or growing more food. Working together in this way, they can achieve a lot.

▷ Rafts on the Rio Grande used to carry fruit and vegetables. Now they carry tourists.

▽ Jamaica's future depends on its young people.

Jamaica

Glossary

Church school A school run by a particular religion.

Colonists Groups of settlers or planters who left their own homes to live in new lands under the rule of their old countries.

Commute To travel to work.

Culture A people's whole way of life. This includes their ideas, beliefs, language, values, knowledge, customs, and the things they make.

Development agency A group or organization set up to improve living conditions for people.

Emigration To move to and settle in another country.

Eviction Being forced to leave a house or building by the owners.

Export Send goods from the home country to other countries.

Fertilizer Chemicals added to the soil to improve its quality, so that more and better plants can be grown.

Import Bring goods into the home country from abroad.

Inflation An increase in prices.

Irrigation A way of providing water for plants using specially built channels and pipes.

Literate Able to read and write.

Minority A small group of people, outnumbered by bigger groups in a population.

Mural A wall painting.

Numerate Able to do basic mathematics.

Patriotic Proud of one's country.

Primary health care Basic health awareness and education that aims to keep people healthy, instead of just curing them when they are ill.

Reggae A type of music with a heavy bass beat, first played in Jamaica and made world famous by Bob Marley.

Sanitation Drains and sewers.

Scholarship Payment by a school or university for the education of a student who shows high ability in a particular subject.

Seasonal Closely connected to a time of year, such as seasonal rains or spring flowers.

Smelt To extract metal from a rock by melting it.

Society How people live as a group and behave towards each other.

Suburb The outer part of a large town or city.

Tradition A belief or custom passed on from one generation to the next.

Unemployment Not having a job.

Union A group of workers who can get better wages and working conditions by acting together, rather than as individuals.

Vaccination An injection that gives protection against certain diseases.

West Indies The islands of the Caribbean, given that name because when Christopher Columbus arrived in the Caribbean, he thought he had reached India.

Index

About Oxfam in Jamaica

Oxfam America works in partnership with communities in Asia, Africa, the Americas, and the Caribbean to find long term solutions to poverty and hunger. Oxfam America supports the self-help efforts of poor people—especially women, landless farm workers, and survivors of war and natural disasters—who are working to make their lives better. Oxfam America believes that all people have the basic rights to earn a living and to have food, shelter, health care, and education.

Oxfam America is part of the international family of Oxfam organizations that work in more than 70 countries, including Jamaica, where Oxfam's program concentrates mainly on rural areas, focusing on strengthening community groups, small farmers' associations, and women's groups. Work includes support to farm cooperatives, which are encouraging farmers to share services to increase yields. A key element in Oxfam's work in Jamaica is "rural animation," that is, encouraging and inspiring community organizations to examine their situations and seek solutions to the problems they identify. In urban areas, Oxfam funds health education programs and again works through local organizations to help poor communities become more aware of what their rights are and how they might obtain them.

© 1996 Rigby Education
Published by Rigby Interactive Library,
an imprint of Rigby Education,
division of Reed Elsevier, Inc.
500 Coventry Lane
Crystal Lake, IL 60014

Printed in Hong Kong
Designed and produced by Visual Image
Cover design by Threefold Design

00 99 98 97 96
10 9 8 7 6 5 4 3 2 1

Library of Congress Cataloging-in-Publication Data

Barraclough, John, 1960-
Jamaica / John Barraclough.
p.   cm. -- (Worldfocus)
Includes index.
Summary: Introduces Jamaica through a geographical and historical profile and case studies of individuals and of a representative community.
ISBN 1-57572-030-2 (lib. bdg.)
1. Jamaica--Juvenile literature.   [1. Jamaica.]
I. Title. II. Series.
F1868.2.B37 1996
972.92--dc20   95-25030

Acknowledgments
The author and publishers would like to thank the following for their help with this book: Oxfam (UK and Ireland): Valerie Cornwall of Oxfam's Jamaican office; Larry Boyd, Latin America and Caribbean Communications officer; Alison Brownlie, Education Advisor; the Williams family of Norwood; Tracey Hawkins of Oxfam's photo library; and, not least, Owen "O.G." Davis.

The author and publishers wish to acknowledge, with thanks, the following photographic sources:

Jamaica Tourist Board pp. 3, 29r; Nancy Durrell-McKenna pp. 4, 5, 8, 9, 11, 12, 15, 16, 17, 19, 20, 21, 22, 23, 24, 28; Belinda Coote p. 6; Neil Cooper pp. 7, 27; John Barraclough pp. 10, 13, 14, 18, 25, 26, 28r.

Every effort has been made to contact copyright holders of material published in this book. Any omissions will be rectified in subsequent printings if notice is given to the publisher.

Cover photograph: Oxfam/Nancy Durrell-McKenna